Embrace Today!

Keepsake Gift Book

A Gift For:

_____

From:

_____

Today, I will be strong and face every obstacle with the courage of a lion.

I will see the beauty in the world around me with every step I take!

I will paint my own picture.

Today, I will not let anyone hold me back from being the most beautiful person I can be!

I will just be me!

I will make no excuses.
I'll reach for the mountaintop,
no matter how hard it is to climb.

Today, I will remember that I can make the world a better place by living every moment with passion, passion to learn from others who have traveled further in life than I.

I will understand
that obstacles are not
barriers for growth, but
opportunities to grow.

I will remember that
even during the storm,
there's joy to be found
in the raindrops.

Today, I will be patient and know that life's most glorious moments are not scripted.

I will do what makes
me happy.

I will believe in myself
and not look for the
approval of others.

Today, I will create
new memories that I
will cherish for the
rest of my life.

I will write an amazing new page in the most important story of all . . . my story!

I will try to leave the
world a better place
than when I found it,
by loving the Earth.

Today, I will learn something
new that I never would
have learned otherwise.

I will slow down
and appreciate the
art of balance.

I will celebrate
transformation and the
beauty of change.

Today, I will let the winds of life guide me to inner peace and meditation.

I will nourish the
world around me with
happiness and hope.

I will stay true to my roots and stand grounded, no matter what comes my way.

Today, I will savor the small comforts and tiny joys that surround me.

I will find beauty in the world around me, and admire and cherish the most delicate moments life has to offer.

I will try to make at least one person smile, and I will spread laughter wherever I can.

Today, I will be the guiding light for others who need it.

I will use my heart as
my compass and follow
it to true North.

I will appreciate the ebbs and flows of life, trusting that it is bigger than what I can see.

Today, I will rise above
my worries and see things
from a higher perspective.

I will trust that I have the
strength to cross any distance.

Today, I will let my inner flame shine brightly to light my path forward.

Today will be my
favorite day!

Images from Shutterstock.com: The Len (3); Enez Selvi (5); Uswatun des (6-7); Muhammadphotoes (9);
Iryna Kalamurza (10-11); Binkgo (13); Pavel_Klimenko (15); Baurzhan I (17); Nejron Photo (19); Denis Belitsky
(20-21); Gordon Magee (23); Violeta Honksisz (25); Aleksandr Ozerov (27); LedyX (28-29); Romolo Tavani
(31); PHOTOCREO Michal Bednarek (33); Najm Shihabi (35); hlphoto (37); muratart (39); Alexander Raths (41);
venars.original (43); sunfe (45); Sakarin Sawasdinaka (47); Rita_Kochmarjova (49); Sadako Desu 22 (50-51);
Aleksey Matrenin (53); icemanphotos (54-55); muratart (57); CK Foto (58-59); kati36 (61); AppleEyesStudio (63).

ISBN 978-1-4971-0560-7

Library of Congress Control Number: 2024925202

To learn more about the other great books from Fox Chapel Publishing, or to find a retailer near you,
call toll-free 800-457-9112, or visit us at www.FoxChapelPublishing.com.

You can also send mail to:
903 Square Street
Mount Joy, PA 17552.

We are always looking for talented authors. To submit an idea, please send a brief inquiry to
acquisitions@foxchapelpublishing.com.

Printed in China

First printing